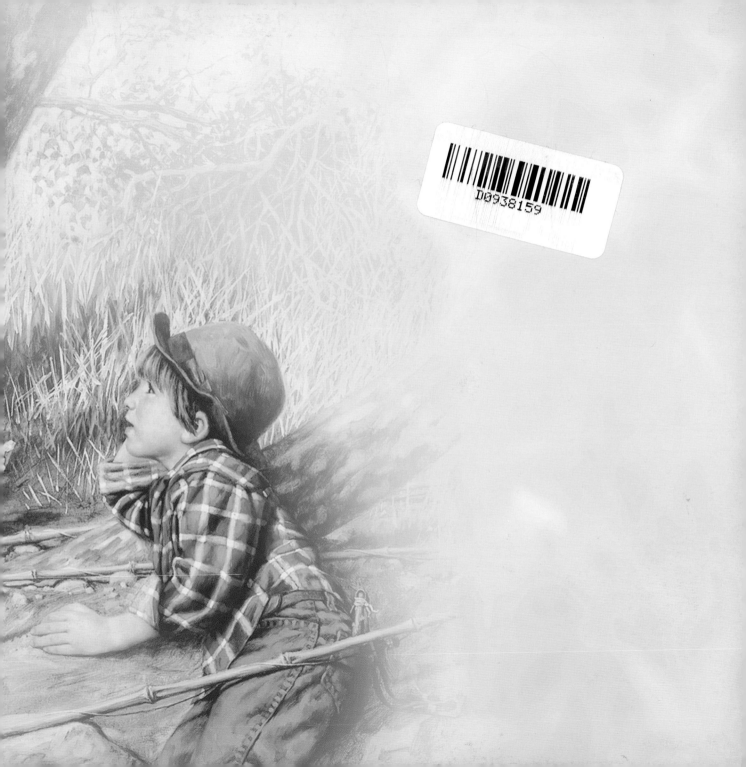

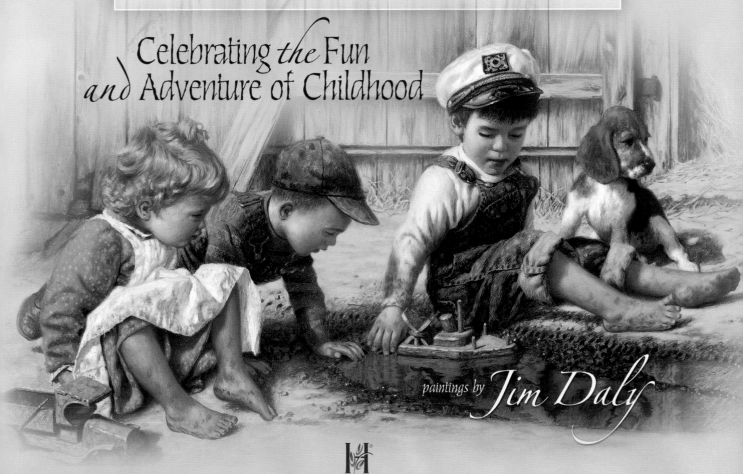

What Little Kids Are Made Of

Celebrating *the* Fun *and* Adventure of Childhood

paintings by *Jim Daly*

HARVEST HOUSE PUBLISHERS

EUGENE, OREGON

What Little Kids Are Made Of

Formerly *Remember When*
Text copyright © 2002 by Harvest House Publishers
Eugene, Oregon 97402

ISBN 0-7369-1602-4

Artwork © by Jim Daly and may not be reproduced without permission. For more
information regarding art prints featured in this book, please contact:

Jim Daly
P.O. Box 25146
Eugene, OR 97402
email: caroledaly@comcast.net

Design and Production by Koechel Peterson & Associates, Inc., Minneapolis, Minnesota

Harvest House Publishers has made every effort to trace the ownership of all poems
and quotes. In the event of a question arising from the use of a poem or quote, we
regret any error made and will be pleased to make the necessary correction in future
editions of this book.

Verses are taken from: The Holy Bible: New International Version®. NIV®. Copyright
© 1973, 1978, 1984 by the International Bible Society. Used by permission of Zondervan
Publishing House. And *The Living Bible*, Copyright © 1971. Used by permission of
Tyndale House Publishers, Inc., Wheaton, Illinois 60189. All rights reserved.

Printed in China

05 06 07 08 09 10 11 12 13 14 / IM / 10 9 8 7 6 5 4 3 2 1

A child's life has no dates;
it is free, silent, dateless.
A child's life ought to be a
child's life, full of simplicity.

OSWALD CHAMBERS

I remember when
an evening on the tire swing
felt a bit like going to church.

I remember, I remember
Where I used to swing,
And thought the air must rush as fresh
To swallows on the wing.

THOMAS HOOD

You could ride in the sky when you saddled and tamed the backyard tire swing. It was as though you had discovered the secrets of angels' wings. And you knew, you just knew that with the right number of swings, the roped tire would carry you beyond the limbs of the apple tree.

Every muscle worked in unison. Taut and lax. Creating more and more air between you and the anthills below. Why was it that time stopped when you became a pendulum in motion? With the view of heaven passing before you, you took the opportunity to talk to God. You thanked Him for the creation of summer evenings and playtime before dinner.

It took focused attention to forge a path in the night sky. But eventually your mother's pursed lips formed the one sound that could pierce your suspended world. With a flushed face, calloused hands, and a dizzy head, your feet became reacquainted with earth. And upon entering the warm, yellow kitchen, you informed your mother that you had spent another evening soaring with God.

GETTING LOST IN THE PRESENCE OF GOD IS A

SACRED HAPPENING, AND IT CAN TAKE PLACE

DURING THE SIMPLEST OF MOMENTS.

Jim Daly

I remember when Father's advice made me a better man.

It didn't matter that I was the best marble shooter on the playground. Or the best speller in my fifth-grade class. I was upset that my cousin Hadley, born just days before me, was a good five inches taller and noticeably stronger. I was convinced that I should be Hadley's physical equal. I began the rigorous training required to initiate an after-school wrestling match: one hundred sit-ups upon rising each morning, fifty push-ups before every meal, fifteen prayers for courage before bedtime.

When Father caught wind of my ambitions, he gave me a good talkin'-to. Father said Hadley was strong and simple and one of the nicest kin we had in our town. And didn't it make good sense to keep Hadley as a friend, seeing as how my mouth made plenty of enemies on a good day?

Next day, I was Hadley's best friend. After school we got an ice cream together and talked about good things: our favorite baseball players of all time, the silliness of girls, and how our town was boring except during the county fair. I put my arm around Hadley's shoulders and felt their mass. And I knew right then, I would be a lucky man if I ended up as smart as Father.

A PARENT'S LIFE-WISDOM, WHEN SHARED, BECOMES

THE FOUNDATION FOR A CHILD'S SUCCESS IN LIFE.

Teach a child to
choose the right path,
And when he is older
he will remain upon it.

THE BOOK OF PROVERBS

Think happy thoughts, O friend, in sunny weather!
Let gladness and thy spirit, hand in hand,
Wander across the daisied fields together
And drink the cheer and sweetness of the land.
So rich a store of memories thou shalt gather…

CHARLES POOLE CLEAVES

Sing it lightly—sing it low—

Sing it softly—like the lisping of the lips we used to know

When our baby-laughter spilled

From the glad hearts ever filled

With music blithe as robin ever trilled!

Let the fragrant summer breeze,

And the leaves of locust-trees,

And the apple-buds and blossoms, and the wings of honey-bees,

All palpitate with glee,

Till the happy harmony

Brings back each childish joy to you and me.

JAMES WHITCOMB RILEY

You are told a lot about your education, but some beautiful, sacred memory, preserved since childhood, is perhaps the best education of all. If a man carries many such memories into life with him, he is saved for the rest of his days.

FYODOR DOSTOYEVSKY

I remember when
listening to the World Series on the radio
was almost as good as being there.

Lou Gehrig, Joe DiMaggio, and the rest of the New York Yankee lineup won the 1937 World Series against the New York Giants. And you saw it all. Every pitch. Every hit. Every run.

In the dining room of your childhood home, your homework was strewn out on the table as a prop, just in case your mother should come by to check on you. Your older brothers claimed to be finished with their homework so they could listen to the game. That plan backfired when Mother declared the supper table as the only place fit for a young man to focus on book learning. They were out. You were in. And the Iron Horse was up to bat.

Funny how the imagination can roll out an entire ball field in the confines of a dining room. And how a seven-year-old boy in Ohio can witness history's finest examples of athleticism while feigning scholarly discipline.

WHEN WE RETURN TO THE IMAGINATION

OF OUR YOUTH, WE GET A BETTER VIEW OF

THE WORLD AS IT SHOULD BE.

Now I lay me down to sleep,
I pray Thee Lord, Thy child to keep;
Thy love go with me all the night
And wake me with the morning light.

AUTHOR UNKNOWN

I remember when
a bedtime story was a cure-all.

The weight of handmade quilts gave you a hug of security, and you sank more deeply into the large bed. Your hint of a cold was soothed by a cup of honey-infused tea that your older sister willingly prepared and served to you.

Your gathering of stuffed animals and handmade dolls snuggled beside you. They too nearly disappeared in the soft down pillows. You settled in to hear a bedtime story. It was such a treat to have your graceful older sister take such time with you. Your sniffles subsided and your body relaxed at the sound of her clear voice.

Only a few books graced the bedside table. Each volume had been passed among the four older children in the family, and now it was your turn. Favorite passages were marked with four-leaf clovers, strands of yarn, and the occasional creased corner. Whether the spoken words conveyed tales of adventure, love, or captivating Bible stories, their rhythm lulled you to sleep.

In today's busyness, how we spend the last moments of our day becomes a significant ritual.

STORIES READ OUT LOUD, QUIET TALKS WITH OUR CHILDREN

AND LOVED ONES, AND PRAYERS OF THANKSGIVING LIFTED UP

TO THE KEEPER OF OUR DAYS...THESE ARE THE TRADITIONS

THAT SOOTHE THE SOUL AT EVERY AGE.

Tom kissed the red lips and said: "Now it's done, Becky. And always after this, you know, you ain't ever to marry anybody but me."

"No, I'll never love anybody but you, Tom, and I'll never marry anybody but you—and you ain't to ever marry anybody but me, either."

"Certainly. Of course. That's part of it. And always coming to school or when we're going home, you're to walk with me, when there ain't anybody looking— and you choose me and I choose you at parties, because that's the way you do when you're engaged."

MARK TWAIN
The Adventures of Tom Sawyer

...and so I follow with my eyes
Where some boy, with a girl upon his arm,
Passes a patch of silver...and I feel
Somehow, I wish I had a woman too,
Walking with little steps under the moon,
And holding my arm so, and smiling.

EDMOND ROSTAND

I remember when the simplest gifts made life richer.

On the morning of your seventh birthday you awakened to the sound of your family gathering at the breakfast table. Everyone greeted you with a kiss on the cheek and a piece of licorice for your pocket. A large, wrapped package awaited you at your place setting. To everyone's surprise, you asked to eat your breakfast first. It was the grown-up thing to do, you said. As you finished every bite of the oatmeal, your gaze never left the present.

The red satin ribbon curled around your fingers as the paper fell to the floor. Peeking from within the box was the smiling face of a handmade fabric doll. You loved her immediately, and she loved you. Her red and blue ribbon hair matched her freshly pressed dress, which was identical to your own Sunday best.

Later, when the tune of the ice-cream wagon sounded throughout the house, Dad reached into his pocket and handed you two shiny pennies. Never again would your brothers be put in charge of carrying your ice-cream money.

On your return walk, you stopped every four steps to take a lick of the ice-cream cone. And with each savored moment, you knew that life as a grown-up was definitely worth waiting for.

TODAY, OUR LIVES ARE FILLED WITH DELICIOUS MOMENTS, EXPERIENCES, AND PLEASURES. MAY WE NEVER FORGET WHAT IT MEANS TO TASTE THE SWEET THINGS IN LIFE, LIKE PRALINE-MAPLE SWIRL AND INDEPENDENCE.

Happy times and bygone
days are never lost...
In truth, they grow more
wonderful within the
heart that keeps them.

KAY ANDREW

Fond Memory brings the light
Of other days around me:
The smiles, the tears
Of boyhood's years.
THOMAS MOORE

Where the hazel bank is steepest,

Where the shadow falls the deepest,

Where the clustering nuts fall free,

That's the way for Billy and me.

Why the boys should drive away

Little sweet maidens from the play,

Or love to banter and fight so well,

That's the thing I never could tell.

But this I know, I love to play

Through the meadow, among the hay;

Up the water and over the lea,

That's the way for Billy and me.

JAMES HOGG

I remember when family time was a part of everyday life.

A warm spring evening was a good excuse for your family to gather on the front porch. Mama played "this little piggy" with your toes while Papa read the paper aloud. The chores for the day were done, and the promise of an evening breeze lingered in the air.

Your dramatic retelling of the day's events sparked your parents' eyes with enthusiasm. It didn't matter that today's account sounded a lot like the one you told yesterday. They teased you when you mentioned the neighbor boy...and *sighed*. But you didn't mind, because their laughter led to stories of when Papa courted the lovely new girl in town, years ago, on this very porch.

The smell of pot roast and creamed corn wafted from the kitchen window and beckoned you all inside. "Just in time," Mama said, her face flush with embarrassment. The three of you gathered around the table and said the blessing. With one eye open, you noticed how their hands fit together perfectly. The safety of their love encircled you and your dreams of the family you would have some day. "Amen," you all said in unison. Amen.

THE HERITAGE OF A LOVING FAMILY IS PASSED ALONG WITH ACTS OF KINDNESS, PATIENCE, AND GOODNESS. WHEN WE LISTEN TO ONE ANOTHER AND TAKE PLEASURE IN EACH OTHER'S OFFERINGS, WE PRESERVE THE LEGACY OF OUR OWN STORY.

Blessed are those
who dwell
in your house;
they are ever
praising you.

THE BOOK OF PSALMS

21

I pledge allegiance to the flag of the United
States of America and to the Republic for
which it stands, one nation under God,
indivisible, with liberty and justice for all.

FRANCIS M. BELLAMY

O sweet and blessed country,

The home of God's elect!

O sweet and blessed country,

That eager hearts expect!

Jesus, in mercy bring us,

To that dear land of rest;

Who art, with God the Father,

And Spirit, ever blest.

BERNARD OF MORLAIX

I remember when handmade clothes
were symbols of love and pride.

On my wedding day, as a young bride of 20, my hands trembled while my mother's steady fingers stitched the last pearls onto my silk dress. The dress had been her mother's. And with hours of measuring, cutting, and tapering, she had transformed it into the dress of my dreams. I stood tall on the stool, high above my kneeling mother. The recollection of this scene from yesteryear took my breath away.

When I was a young, growing girl, Mother would change out the hem on my dresses each fall. With creative touches, she made the dresses longer, brighter, and more refined. Some years, there would be added lace or shiny new buttons, specially ordered from the Sears & Roebuck catalog. Even as a child I knew that her attention to every detail was her way of making up for our large family's limited resources.

Now, as I prepared for the most significant day of my life, I had the resources for a pristine white "something new." But the dress that draped my body, and made me feel like a princess, was far finer. I was wearing a garment stitched with the golden threads of love.

THE SMALLEST GESTURES, THE SIMPLEST ACTS OF LOVE—

THEY ARE THE TREASURES THAT SHINE BRILLIANTLY IN ONE'S MEMORY,

FOR THEY ARE THE MOMENTS THAT HAVE INSPIRED YOUR

OWN EFFORTS AT KINDNESS EVER SINCE.

Memories of our lives,
of our works and our deeds
will continue in others.

ROSA PARKS

It is threads,
hundreds of tiny threads,
which sew people together
through the years.

SIMONE SIGNORET

25

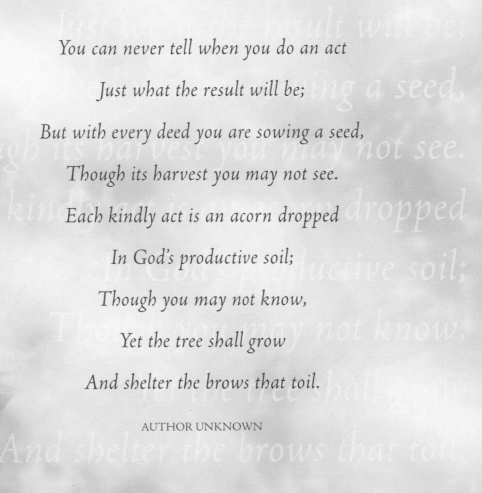

You can never tell when you do an act

Just what the result will be;

But with every deed you are sowing a seed,

Though its harvest you may not see.

Each kindly act is an acorn dropped

In God's productive soil;

Though you may not know,

Yet the tree shall grow

And shelter the brows that toil.

AUTHOR UNKNOWN

A wise teacher makes learning a joy.

THE BOOK OF PROVERBS

When thy heart with joy o'erflowing
Sings a thankful prayer,
In thy joy, O let thy brother
With thee share.

THEODORE CHICKERING WILLIAMS

THE BAREFOOT BOY

Blessings on thee, little man,

Barefoot boy, with cheek of tan!

With thy turned-up pantaloons,

And thy merry whistled tunes;

With thy red lip, redder still

Kissed by strawberries on the hill;

With the sunshine on thy face,

Through thy torn brim's jaunty grace;

From my heart I give thee joy,—

I was once a barefoot boy!

JOHN GREENLEAF WHITTIER

I remember when
my little sister became my friend.

On Sundays, as soon as Mom would start preparing apples for our evening pie, my little sister and I headed for the neighboring field. We waved to Ronnie, the aging horse that rarely looked up from his eternal grazing, and we slipped between the tattered wooden fences. We were very careful not to catch the hem of our dresses; the slightest tear became incriminating evidence of such escapades. This we had learned.

Our games of tag through the neck-high wildflowers left us breathless and giggling. While we rested, I blew dandelion seeds into the air, high above my sister's grasping fingers. With her head bent back and her mouth wide open, her laughter rose above the cotton wisps and startled Ronnie mid-chew.

The same sister who bothered me with her omnipresence and constant chatter was, in moments like this, angelic. I still remember how her hair smelled of sunshine and creek water as we twirled together in that field, and how our shared language of joy was imprinted on our hearts forever.

THE SOUND OF OUR HAPPINESS TODAY ECHOES

WITH OUR CHILDHOOD LAUGHTER.

How dear to this heart
are the scenes of my
childhood, when fond
recollection recalls them
to view; the orchard, the
meadow, the deep-tangled
wildwood, and every
loved spot, which my
infancy knew.

SAMUEL WOODWORTH

Jim Daly

I remember when my new dog introduced me to the cool boys.

I stood on the edge of the playground hoping it was my day to be noticed by a certain group of boys. Accepted. Invited to the next round of marbles. But I played only the role of observer. I had not yet been allowed to cross over the invisible line between them and me. That is, until the day Rascal changed everything.

My dad discovered the dog one night at the railroad. His fur was tangled in patches of sap and pine needles. The other workmen deemed the canine "a mess of a dog." But my father recognized a gentle loyalty in the dog and brought him home to me.

Deciding on a proper name was my task at hand. I thought long and hard throughout the day and was still stumped as the nameless dog and I headed home after school. Then we spotted the group of boys. Robby Pinski had a clean shot lined up to take Johnny Henderson's last blue marble when the leash left my hands, and I watched, horrified, as my new friend barreled into the sacred circle.

In the funnel of dirt that was my dog, marbles flew, Robby Pinski tumbled, and Johnny Henderson quickly called for a rematch between fits of laughter. "What is your dog's name?!" Robby demanded. "Uh…Rascal…he is Rascal," I improvised. "He sure is," laughed Johnny. "And I think we just got ourselves an official mascot. What do you say, fellas?"

And just like that, the circle was made big enough to include me and my dog, Rascal.

WHEN WE GIVE OR ARE GIVEN THE NAME "FRIEND," OUR CIRCLE OF

BLESSING EXPANDS AND BECOMES FAR MORE SIGNIFICANT.

Thus the little minutes,
Humble though they be,
Make the mighty ages
Of eternity.

JULIE FLETCHER CARNEY

A child's cravings for sweets
is a call of nature. It is
necessary to the proper
development of their bodies.

LAURA INGALLS WILDER

I scream,
You scream,
We all scream
For ice cream.

AUTHOR UNKNOWN

And every day, little Charlie Bucket,

trudging through the snow on his way to school,

would have to pass Mr. Willy Wonka's

giant chocolate factory. And every day,

as he came near to it, he would lift his small

pointed nose high in the air and sniff the wonderful

sweet smell of melting chocolate. Sometimes, he would

stand motionless outside the gates for several minutes

on end, taking deep swallowing breaths as though

he were trying to eat the smell itself.

ROALD DAHL
Charlie and the Chocolate Factory

Little Brook—laugh and leap!
Do not let the dreamer weep:
Sing him all the songs of summer till he sink in softest sleep;
And then sing soft and low
Through his dreams of long ago—
Sing back to him the rest he used to know!

JAMES WHITCOMB RILEY

Oh, I have a little brook,

That mother doesn't know;

Ev'ry day I come to look,

Because I love it so.

All alone I run away

To my brook here in the dell

And together we two play

Until the supper bell.

WILLIAM NORTHRUP MORSE

Delight and liberty, the simple creed of
Childhood, whether busy or at rest...

WILLIAM WORDSWORTH

Jim Daly

The foolish fears of what might pass,
I cast them all away
Among the clover-scented grass,
Among the new-mown hay,
Among the husking of the corn,
Where drowsy poppies nod
Where ill thoughts die and good are born—
Out in the fields with God.

AUTHOR UNKNOWN

I remember when I discovered that nature made for pretty good company.

The wind met you that day in the field. The day your older brother headed out to go fishing before you even woke up.

He left the dogs behind because they were "too much trouble" on such an outing. You suspected the same was mumbled about you.

When you said that you envied your brother's solo adventure, your mother returned from the kitchen with a packed lunch, just like the one she had prepared for your brother. *You* took the dogs because you sympathized with them. And you headed out on your own.

The sky was dark; yet brief moments of sun cast a spotlight on your piece of the field. Your kite soared without the least bit of resistance. It too had been so ready to greet the wind. You let your thoughts fly high and free. As you told the dogs about your dreams of becoming an aviator some day, they grinned with approval.

Soon it was time to reel the kite in and head for home. Over dinner, your brother, between big bites of sweet potatoes, talked about how fun it was to get lost in nature and how free he felt when he stood alone under a stormy sky. "You just don't understand," he said when you laughed out loud. Little did he know, you too had discovered nature's sacred friendship that day.

SELF-DISCOVERY IS REALLY ABOUT UNCOVERING THE GIFTS FROM GOD THAT LIE WITHIN YOUR OWN SOUL. AND AS EACH GIFT IS UNCOVERED ALONG LIFE'S PATH, STRENGTH, HOPE, AND PROMISE GIVE BREATH TO EACH NEW DAY.

When the lessons and tasks are all ended,
And the school for the day is dismiss'd,
And the little ones gather around me,
To bid me good-night and be kiss'd:
Oh, the little white arms that encircle
My neck in a tender embrace!
Oh, the smiles that are halos of heaven,
Shedding sunshine of love on my face!

CHARLES M. DICKINSON

Child heart,

Wild heart!

What can I bring you,

What can I sing you,

You have come from a glory afar,

Called into Time from a secret star?

…Mad thing,

Glad thing!

How will Life tame you?

How will God name you?

All that I know is that you are to me

Wind over water, star on the sea.

EDWIN MARKHAM

I remember when…

The Smith boys, Frankie, Will, and Samuel, played stickball with every ounce of energy young lads could muster on a hot August afternoon. They made sure nobody stole base. They swung hard. And they dove into the dirt whenever it made a good show. But their eyes all darted to the road with anticipation. And their ears were tuned-in to hear their little sister's shrill announcement, "He's coming! He's coming!"

The iceman, Fred, turned the corner and honked twice. All play stopped as the boys ran to meet the wagon. They stood patiently as Fred used the large steel clamps to grab a block of ice, hoist it to his shoulder, and make his first delivery. They waited. With tongues stuck to the roofs of dry mouths, they waited.

Fred returned to see them lined up like ducklings. "You're all still here? Now, what on earth could you be waiting for?" He smiled at his part in the routine. "Aw, Fred!" They cried in unison. "Only for you, fellas. Only for you." He beamed as he reached into the wagon and struck a partial block of ice with a long pick. Those closest felt the spray on their faces. One by one, they received chips of ice. Some pieces as large as their hands!

The boys waved goodbye to Fred, who headed on to the houses by Whitaker Grove—where the Fletcher boys were playing stickball, watching the road, and listening for their little sister's shrill announcement, "He's coming! He's coming!"

MEMORIES OF CHILDHOOD ANTICIPATION AND PLEASURE SERVE

UP PURE REFRESHMENT WHEN RECALLED LATER IN LIFE.

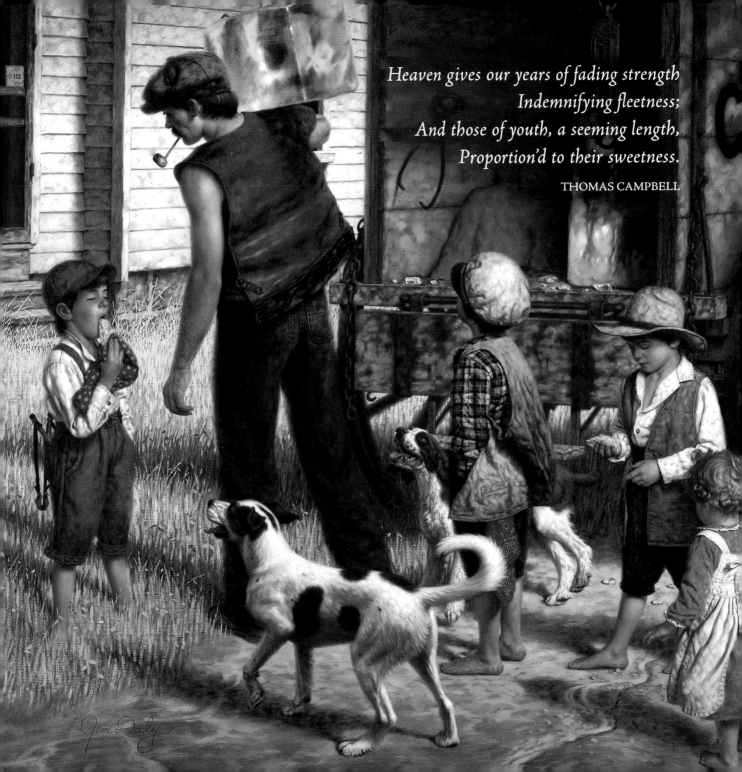

Heaven gives our years of fading strength
Indemnifying fleetness;
And those of youth, a seeming length,
Proportion'd to their sweetness.

THOMAS CAMPBELL

Children, sing! who can tell
If the song you love so well,
May not reach one whose heart
Longs to choose the better part?
Stealing soft, like the sigh
Of a zephyr passing by,
Children, sing, ever sing,
Loudest praise to God our King.

FANNY CROSBY

And she ran into the middle of the room and, taking a handle in each hand, began to skip, and skip, and skip, while Mary turned in her chair to stare at her, and the queer faces in the old portraits seemed to stare at her, too, and wonder what on earth this common little cottager had the impudence to be doing under their very noses. But Martha did not even see them. The interest and curiosity in Mistress Mary's face delighted her, and she went on skipping and counted as she skipped until she had reached a hundred.

FRANCES HODGSON BURNETT

The Secret Garden

45

He who gives a child a book,
Gives that child a sweeping look,
Through its pages
Down the ages.

Gives that child a ship to sail,
Where the far adventurers hail
Down the sea
Of destiny.

Gives that child great dreams to dream;
Sun-lit ways that glint and gleam
Where the sages
Tramp the ages.

WILLIAM L. STIDGER

I remember when I was a ship's captain.

Every waking moment and every minute of deep slumber was filled with dreams of what you would become some day. Most certainly your life would not consist of milking cows and staying after school to clean chalkboards as punishment for being tardy! No, there would be much more adventure involved. The great sea your grandfather spoke of with such longing would someday be your home.

The rise and fall of waves would carry you to new worlds. The vastness of God's oceans would be filled with wonders. You would study creatures of the sea. You would examine the night's stars to calculate your journey through the deep waters. Then you would return home after months away and share news of discovered lands and magnificent treasure. And your teacher would tell students how she had once disciplined the famous local hero when he was just a young, restless boy in coveralls.

YOU STILL DREAM OF WHAT YOU WILL ONE DAY BECOME.
AND WITH EACH PASSING FANCY, THOSE WHO BELIEVE IN
YOU ALONG THE WAY WITH UNWAVERING FAITH BECOME
THE CORNERSTONE OF YOUR HOPE FOR TOMORROW.

Jim Daly

Memory is not just the
imprint of the past upon us;
it is the keeper of what is
meaningful for our deepest hopes.

ROLLO MAY